101 SUPER-EASY
Slow-Cooker RECIPES

Slow-Cooked Veggie-Beef Soup, page 70   *Chinese 5-Spice Chicken, page 43*   *Slow-Cooker Sausage-Stuffed Peppers, page 94*

Gooseberry Patch

An imprint of Globe Pequot
246 Goose Lane
Guilford, CT 06437

www.gooseberrypatch.com
1·800·854·6673

Copyright 2013, Gooseberry Patch 978-1-62093-090-8

Gooseberry Patch
cookbooks

Paprika Beef & Noodles, page 53

Brunswick Stew, page 40

Since 1992, we've been publishing our own country cookbooks for every kitchen and for every meal of the day! Each title has hundreds of budget-friendly recipes, using ingredients you already have on hand in your pantry.

In addition, you'll find helpful tips and ideas on every page, along with our hand-drawn artwork and plenty of personality. Their lay-flat binding makes them so easy to use...they're sure to become a fast favorite in your kitchen.

Call us toll-free at
1•800•854•6673
and we'd be delighted to tell you all about our newest titles!

Shop with us online anytime at
www.gooseberrypatch.com

Honeyed Apple Treat, page 89

Cranberry Kielbasa Bites, page 29

Susan's Slow-Cookin' Ribs, page 62

Chicken Tortilla Soup, page 63

Garden-Style Fettuccine, page 14

Spicy Carnitas Tacos, page 93

Perfect Pumpkin-Apple Cake, page 27

CONTENTS

Italian Meatball Subs, page 79

Dedication

For every cook who loves letting the slow cooker do the work while they're away!

Appreciation

Thank you to all those amazing cooks who shared their slow-cooker favorites...this one's for you.

Teriyaki Pork Roast, page 45

Chipotle-Black Bean Dip

16-oz. can refried beans
15-oz. can black beans, drained
  and rinsed
11-oz. can sweet corn & diced
  peppers, drained
1 c. chunky salsa
2 chipotle chiles in adobo sauce,
  chopped and 2 t. adobo sauce
  reserved
1-1/2 c. shredded Cheddar
  cheese
4 green onions, chopped
tortilla chips

Mix together beans, corn, salsa,
chiles, reserved adobo sauce and
one cup cheese in a slow cooker.
Cover and cook on low setting for
3 to 4 hours, stirring after 2 hours.
Sprinkle with remaining cheese and
onions. Keep warm on low setting;
serve with tortilla chips. Makes
12 servings.

Vickie
I am always asked to take
this smoky, spicy bean dip
wherever I go...I've even
started bringing the recipe
to share.

Roasted Cajun Pecans

1 t. chili powder
1 t. dried basil
1 t. dried oregano
1 t. dried thyme
1 t. salt
1/2 t. onion powder
1/2 t. garlic powder
1/4 t. cayenne pepper
1/4 c. butter, melted
1 lb. pecan halves

In a small bowl, mix together spices. Pour melted butter into a slow cooker; stir in pecans until evenly coated. Sprinkle spice mixture over pecans, stirring constantly, until evenly seasoned. Cover and cook on high setting for 12 to 15 minutes, stirring once. Remove lid from slow cooker and reduce heat to low setting. Cook, uncovered, for 2 hours, stirring occasionally. Remove pecans from slow cooker; cool on a paper towel-lined wire rack. Makes 8 servings.

Becky Butler
Keller, TX

When pecans start falling from their trees in September and October, it's the perfect time to roast them for snacking!

Tex-Mex Taco Joes

3 lbs. ground beef, browned
  and drained
16-oz. can refried beans
10-oz. can enchilada sauce
1-1/4 oz. pkg. taco seasoning mix
16-oz. jar salsa
25 hot dog buns, split
Garnish: shredded Cheddar
  cheese, shredded lettuce,
  chopped tomatoes, sour cream

Place beef in a slow cooker. Stir in
beans, enchilada sauce, seasoning
mix and salsa. Cover and cook
on low setting for 4 to 6 hours.
To serve, fill each bun with 1/3 cup
beef mixture; garnish as desired.
Makes 25 sandwiches.

9

**Sherry Cress
Salem, IN**

A super-simple meal that's
   full of flavor. Try
garnishing with a little
peach or pineapple salsa...
      really good!

Parsley Buttered Potatoes

1-1/2 lbs. new redskin potatoes
1/4 c. water
1/4 c. butter, melted
1 T. lemon juice
3 T. fresh parsley, minced
1 T. fresh chives, snipped
salt and pepper to taste

If desired, pare a strip around the middle of each potato. Place potatoes and water in a slow cooker. Cover and cook on high setting for 2-1/2 to 3 hours, until tender; drain. In a small bowl, combine butter, lemon juice, parsley and chives. Pour over potatoes; toss to coat. Sprinkle with salt and pepper. Serves 6.

Kendall Hale
Lynn, MA

Butter, chives and a dash of lemon juice jump-start this super-easy, super-tasty recipe. These potatoes are perfect for toting to a potluck or get-together.

Root Beer Pulled Pork Sandwiches

2-lb. pork tenderloin
salt and pepper to taste
2 c. root beer
18-oz. bottle favorite barbecue
   sauce
5 to 6 potato rolls, split

Season pork on all sides with salt and pepper. Place pork in a slow cooker; pour root beer over top. Cover and cook on low setting for 4 to 6 hours, until pork is very tender. Remove pork from slow cooker and discard juices. Shred pork and return to slow cooker; stir in barbecue sauce. Serve pork on rolls for sandwiches. Serves 5 to 6.

Sarah Gardner
Schuylerville, NY

My family loves to come home to the smell of this pulled pork simmering away! Since the slow cooker does all the work, we have more time to spend with each other.

Classic Coney Sauce

3 lbs. lean ground beef, browned
  and drained
28-oz. can tomato purée
1 c. onion, chopped
2 T. chili powder
1-1/2 T. mustard
1-1/2 T. Worcestershire sauce
1 T. salt
1 T. pepper
1 t. garlic powder

Combine all ingredients in a slow
cooker. Cover and cook on high
setting for 3 hours, stirring
occasionally. Turn heat to low setting
to keep warm. Makes enough sauce
for about 20 hot dogs.

Cathy Young
Evansville, IN
Makes enough to satisfy
a hungry team of
Little Leaguers!

Hearty Pork & Beans

1 lb. ground beef
1 green pepper, chopped
1 onion, chopped
16-oz. pkg. smoked pork sausage,
    halved lengthwise and thinly
    sliced
16-oz. can pork & beans
15-oz. can lima beans, drained
    and rinsed
15-oz. can pinto beans, drained
    and rinsed
1 c. catsup
1/2 c. brown sugar, packed
1 t. salt
1/2 t. garlic powder
1/4 t. pepper

In a skillet over medium heat, brown beef with green pepper and onion; drain. Add remaining ingredients to a lightly greased slow cooker; stir in beef mixture. Cover and cook on low setting for 4 to 5 hours, until heated through. Serves 8.

Pam Hundley
Port Crane, NY

This quick & easy meal is perfect paired with a thick slice of crusty bread and a salad. When I take it to a BBQ or church potluck, I'm always asked for the recipe.

13

Garden-Style Fettuccine

1 zucchini, sliced 1/4-inch thick
1 yellow squash, sliced 1/4-inch thick
2 carrots, peeled and thinly sliced
1-1/2 c. sliced mushrooms
10-oz. pkg. frozen broccoli cuts
4 green onions, sliced
1 clove garlic, minced
1/2 t. dried basil
1/4 t. salt
1/2 t. pepper
1 c. grated Parmesan cheese
12-oz. pkg. fettuccine pasta, cooked
1 c. shredded mozzarella cheese
1 c. milk
2 egg yolks, beaten

Place vegetables, seasonings and Parmesan cheese in a slow cooker. Cover and cook on high setting for 2 hours. Add remaining ingredients to slow cooker; stir well. Reduce heat to low setting; cover and cook an additional 15 to 30 minutes. Makes 6 to 8 servings.

Lisa Hays
Crocker, MO

What a delicious, nutritious meatless meal! It's packed full of veggies and yummy cheese...what more could you ask for?

Mike's Irresistible Italian Chops

5 pork chops
1-1/2 onions, coarsely chopped
15-oz. can stewed tomatoes
1/3 c. oil
1-1/2 t. Italian seasoning
1-1/2 t. garlic powder
2 t. smoke-flavored cooking
   sauce
1/4 c. water

Layer chops and onions in a slow cooker; add tomatoes with juice and remaining ingredients. Cover and cook on low setting for 3 to 4 hours, until chops are tender. Makes 5 servings.

15

Leslie McKinley
Macomb, MO

My dad is a master at cooking meats, and this is one of his signature dishes! We enjoy these chops with buttered noodles, rice or couscous.

Smashed Redskin Potatoes

5 lbs. redskin potatoes,
   quartered
1 T. garlic, minced
3 cubes chicken bouillon
8-oz. container sour cream
8-oz. pkg. cream cheese,
   softened
1/2 c. butter, softened
salt and pepper to taste

Place potatoes, garlic and bouillon
in a large saucepan; cover with
water. Bring to a boil; cook just
until potatoes are tender, about
15 minutes. Drain, reserving cooking
liquid. Place potatoes, sour cream
and cream cheese in a large bowl;
mash potatoes, adding cooking liquid
as needed until desired consistency is
reached. Spoon into a slow cooker;
cover and cook on low setting for
2 to 3 hours. Stir in butter, salt
and pepper just before serving.
Serves 10 to 12.

Kary Marone
Des Moines, IA
Everyone loves these
potatoes...a nice change from
the same ol' mashed potato.
They're oh-so pretty served
in a big bowl, garnished
with snipped chives.

Fantastic 40-Clove Chicken

4 boneless, skinless
   chicken breasts
2 t. salt
1 t. pepper
40 cloves garlic, peeled
3/4 c. dry white wine or
   chicken broth
1 t. dried thyme
1-1/2 t. dried rosemary
1 bay leaf
1 T. butter

Season chicken with salt and pepper; place in a slow cooker. Add garlic, wine or broth and seasonings to slow cooker. Cover and cook on low setting for 4 to 6 hours, until chicken juices run clear. Remove chicken from slow cooker and pour juices through a strainer, mashing some garlic cloves through as well. Discard bay leaf. Cook juice mixture in a saucepan over high heat until thickened, about 6 to 8 minutes. Add butter to sauce; stir until mixed. Drizzle sauce over chicken. Serves 6 to 8.

17

Amy James
Fayetteville, AR
You'll be amazed at how sweet and flavorful the garlic is after cooking all day. You can usually buy already-peeled garlic in the produce section.

Stewed Black-Eyed Peas

1 lb. dried black-eyed peas
1 lb. andouille pork sausage,
  cut into 1/4-inch slices
1 c. yellow onion, chopped
1/2 t. salt
2 T. hot pepper sauce
5 cloves garlic, pressed
4 bay leaves
1 t. dried thyme
1 t. dried parsley
8 c. chicken broth

Combine all ingredients in a slow cooker. Cover and cook on low setting for 5 to 6 hours. Discard bay leaves before serving. Serves 8 to 10.

Leslie Stimel
Columbus, OH

Andouille is a spicy sausage from Louisiana...perfect for this hearty dish, but you can use another spicy smoked sausage if you like.

Greek Chicken Pitas

1 onion, diced
3 cloves garlic, minced
1 lb. boneless, skinless chicken
   breasts, cut into strips
1 t. lemon-pepper seasoning
1/2 t. dried oregano
1/4 t. allspice
1/4 c. plain yogurt
1/4 c. sour cream
1/2 c. cucumber, peeled and
   diced
4 rounds pita bread, halved
   and split

Place onion and garlic in a slow
cooker; set aside. Sprinkle chicken
with seasonings; add to slow cooker.
Cover and cook on high setting for
6 hours. Meanwhile, stir together
yogurt, sour cream and cucumber in
a small bowl; chill. Fill pita halves
with chicken mixture and drizzle with
yogurt sauce. Makes 4 sandwiches.

19

Peggy Pelfrey
Ashland City, TN

For a real treat, top these
pitas with some crumbled
feta cheese and sliced
black olives.

Dijon-Ginger Carrots

12 carrots, peeled and sliced
   1/4-inch thick
1/3 c. Dijon mustard
1/2 c. brown sugar, packed
1 t. fresh ginger, peeled and
   minced
1/2 t. salt
1/8 t. pepper

Combine all ingredients in a slow cooker; stir. Cover and cook on high setting for 2 to 3 hours, until carrots are tender, stirring twice during cooking. Makes 10 to 12 servings.

Angela Murphy
Tempe, AZ

Tangy mustard and ginger, sweet brown sugar...I just adore this super-simple dressed-up carrot recipe! Sprinkle carrots with a little snipped fresh chives or fresh mint.

Mom's Classic Cabbage Rolls

1-1/2 lbs. ground beef
1/2 c. instant rice, uncooked
1 egg
1 t. garlic powder
1/2 t. salt
1/2 t. pepper
1 onion, diced
12 to 14 cabbage leaves

In a bowl, mix together uncooked beef and remaining ingredients except cabbage leaves; set aside. Drop cabbage leaves into boiling water for 3 to 4 minutes, until pliable; drain. Place 1/4 cup beef mixture in the center of each leaf. Fold in sides and roll up; set aside. Pour half the Tomato Sauce into a slow cooker; add cabbage rolls. Pour remaining sauce over rolls. Cover and cook on high setting for 5 to 6 hours. Serves 4 to 6.

Tomato Sauce:

2 8-oz. cans tomato sauce
juice of 2 lemons
3 T. all-purpose flour
1/2 c. sugar

Combine all ingredients in a bowl; mix well.

Dixie Dill
Elkland, MO

My mom gave me this recipe when I was a frazzled newlywed. It's simple and delicious, especially good on a cold winter day.

21

Divine Seafood Chowder

1 onion, sliced
4 potatoes, peeled and sliced
minced garlic to taste
1 t. dill weed
2 T. butter, diced
1 c. clam juice, heated to boiling
15-oz. can creamed corn
salt and pepper to taste
1/2 lb. haddock or cod fillets
1/2 lb. medium shrimp, peeled,
    cleaned and halved
1 c. light cream, warmed

Layer all ingredients except cream in
a slow cooker, placing fish and
shrimp on top. Cover and cook on
high setting for one hour; reduce
setting to low and cook for 3 hours.
Gently stir in cream just before
serving. Makes 4 to 6 servings.

Audrey Laudenat
East Haddam, CT

This chowder is a meal in
itself. Serve with cornbread
squares, slices of crusty
bread and cold iced
tea...don't forget the
oyster crackers!

Chicken with Artichokes & Capers

3 lbs. boneless, skinless chicken
   thighs
salt and pepper to taste
14-1/2 oz. can diced tomatoes
14-oz. can artichoke hearts,
   drained
1/4 c. capers
2 to 3 cloves garlic, thinly sliced
8-oz. pkg. sliced mushrooms
3 tomatoes, chopped
16-oz. pkg. spaghetti, cooked

Season chicken with salt and pepper;
place in a slow cooker. Spoon canned
tomatoes with juice, artichokes,
capers and garlic over chicken.
Cover and cook on high setting for
3 to 4 hours, until chicken juices
run clear. Stir in fresh tomatoes
and mushrooms during the last
30 minutes of cooking. Serve
chicken and sauce over spaghetti.
Serves 6 to 8.

Sandra Sullivan
Aurora, CT

Quick, easy and a hit with
the whole family! Add a
simple side salad and warm
bread...you'll have a gourmet
dinner in no time.

Pumpkin Patch Soup

2 t. olive oil
1/2 c. raw pumpkin seeds
3 slices thick-cut bacon
1 onion, chopped
1 t. salt
1/2 t. chipotle chili powder
1/2 t. pepper
2 29-oz. cans pumpkin
4 c. chicken broth
3/4 c. apple cider
1/2 c. whipping cream

Heat oil in a small skillet over medium heat. Add pumpkin seeds to oil; cook and stir until seeds begin to pop, about one minute. Remove seeds to a bowl and set aside. Add bacon to skillet and cook until crisp. Remove bacon to a paper towel; crumble and refrigerate. Add onion to drippings in pan. Sauté until translucent, about 5 minutes. Stir in seasonings. Spoon onion mixture into a slow cooker. Whisk pumpkin, broth and cider into onion mixture. Cover and cook on high setting for 4 hours. Whisk in cream. Top servings with pumpkin seeds and crumbled bacon. Serves 4.

Jo Ann

Every fall, my family begs me to make this soup. They like it so much, I've started making it year 'round!

Squash, Chickpea & Lentil Stew

3/4 c. dried chickpeas
2-1/2 lbs. butternut squash, peeled and cut into 1/2-inch cubes
2 carrots, peeled and sliced
1 onion, chopped
1 c. dried red lentils
4 c. vegetable broth
2 T. tomato paste
1 T. fresh ginger, peeled and grated
1-1/2 t. ground cumin
1 t. salt
1/4 t. pepper
1/4 c. lime juice
1/2 c. peanuts, chopped
1/4 c. fresh cilantro, chopped

Place chickpeas in a saucepan and cover with 2 inches of water; let soak overnight. Drain chickpeas and combine with vegetables, lentils, broth, tomato paste, ginger and seasonings in a slow cooker. Cover and cook on low setting for 5 to 6 hours. Stir in lime juice; sprinkle servings with peanuts and cilantro. Serves 8.

Emily Martin
Toronto, Ontario

A healthy and hearty stew, this dish is a staple for us during the chilly winters. Serve with brown rice and you've got a stick-to-your-ribs delight.

25

Candy-Apple Tapioca

8 McIntosh apples, peeled, cored
  and thinly sliced
2/3 c. sugar
1/4 c. instant tapioca, uncooked
3 T. red cinnamon candies
1/2 c. milk
Garnish: whipped cream

Place apples in a lightly greased slow
cooker. In a bowl, stir together sugar,
tapioca, candies and milk. Pour sugar
mixture over apples. Cover and cook
on high setting for 3 to 4 hours. Stir
well before serving. Top servings with
a dollop of whipped cream. Serves 8.

Janis Parr
Campbellford, Ontario
This yummy dessert is really
two delectable desserts
in one...creamy tapioca
pudding and sweet
cinnamon-spiced apples!

Perfect Pumpkin-Apple Cake

1/2 c. butter, softened
1-1/2 c. brown sugar, packed
1 c. canned pumpkin
3 eggs
2 c. all-purpose flour
2 t. baking powder
1/4 t. baking soda
1 t. cinnamon
1/4 t. salt
Optional: chopped walnuts or
    pecans to taste
21-oz. can apple pie filling
12-oz. container frozen whipped
    topping, thawed

In a large bowl, beat together butter and brown sugar with an electric mixer on low speed until well mixed. Beat in pumpkin and eggs until blended. In a separate bowl, sift together flour, baking powder, baking soda, cinnamon and salt. Slowly add flour mixture to butter mixture; beat for 2 minutes. Fold in nuts, if using. Spoon pie filling into a slow cooker; pour batter over pie filling. Cover and cook on high setting for 1-1/2 to 2 hours, until a toothpick tests clean. Garnish servings with a dollop of whipped topping. Serves 8.

Sandra Sullivan
Aurora, CO
No oven needed...so easy to do on the run! This tasty cake is perfect for when your oven is all tied up with other yummy treats.

27

Too-Easy Teriyaki Wings

3/4 c. sugar
1/2 c. brown sugar, packed
1 t. garlic powder
1 t. ground ginger
1 c. soy sauce
3/4 c. water
1/4 c. pineapple juice
1/4 c. oil
4 lbs. chicken wings
Garnish: chopped green onion,
   sesame seeds

In a large bowl, mix together all
ingredients except wings. Add wings;
toss to coat evenly. Cover and
refrigerate at least 2 hours. Remove
wings from marinade; place in a slow
cooker. Pour one cup marinade over
wings; discard remaining marinade.
Cover and cook on low setting for
8 to 9 hours. Garnish with green
onions and sesame seeds before
serving. Serves 4 to 6.

Dwight Rutan
Clinton, OH

I'm a big fan of chicken
wings, so when I found out
I could make them in my slow
cooker, my football-watching
days haven't been the
same since!

Cranberry Kielbasa Bites

2 16-oz. Kielbasa sausage rings,
   cut into 1/2-inch pieces
2 14-oz. pkgs. mini smoked
   sausages
3/4 c. catsup
14-oz. can whole-berry
   cranberry sauce
1/2 c. grape jelly

Place all ingredients in a slow
cooker; stir to mix well. Cover and
cook on low setting for 7 to 8 hours.
Serves 10 to 12.

29

Kelley Annis
Massena, NY

I received this recipe from
a cousin who told me it was
great for get-togethers. Now
I am asked to bring it to
the luncheon at work every
year...it's that good!

Chicken Parmigiana

1 egg
3/4 c. milk
salt and pepper to taste
2 c. Italian-seasoned dry bread
  crumbs
4 boneless, skinless chicken
  breasts
2 T. oil
26-oz. jar spaghetti sauce,
  divided
1 to 2 c. shredded mozzarella
  cheese
cooked spaghetti

Beat together egg and milk in a deep bowl. Add salt and pepper; set aside. Place bread crumbs in a shallow bowl. Dip chicken breasts into egg mixture; coat with crumb mixture. Heat oil in a skillet over medium heat; cook chicken just until golden on both sides. Add one cup sauce to bottom of a slow cooker; top with chicken. Spoon remaining sauce over chicken. Cover and cook on low setting for 6 to 8 hours. About 15 minutes before serving, sprinkle cheese over top; cover until melted. Serve chicken and sauce over cooked spaghetti. Makes 4 servings.

Diane Tracy
Lake Mary, FL

This is incredibly
delicious...so tender you
won't need a knife!

Sweet & Savory Beef Sandwiches

12-oz. can beer or non-alcoholic
 beer
1 c. brown sugar, packed
24-oz. bottle catsup
3 to 4-lb. boneless beef roast
6 to 8 split Kaiser rolls
Optional: banana pepper slices

Stir together beer, sugar and catsup in a slow cooker. Add roast and spoon mixture over top. Cover and cook on low setting for 7 to 8 hours. Remove roast and shred; return to juices in slow cooker. Serve shredded beef on rolls for sandwiches, topped with pepper slices if desired. Serves 6 to 8.

Lisa Schneck
Lehighton, PA

I love the simplicity of my slow cooker...just add ingredients, turn it on, and a few hours later this delicious, no-fuss meal awaits my hungry family.

Slow-Cooker Barbacoa Beef

3 to 4-lb. beef chuck roast
3 bay leaves
1 c. cider vinegar
juice of 2 limes
3 chipotle peppers in
   adobo sauce
4 cloves garlic
1 T. ground cumin
1 T. dried oregano
1-1/2 t. salt
1-1/2 t. pepper
1/2 t. ground cloves
1 c. chicken broth
flour tortillas
Garnish: shredded Colby Jack
   cheese, shredded lettuce,
   guacamole

Place roast and bay leaves in a large slow cooker. In a food processor or blender, combine vinegar, lime juice, peppers, garlic and seasonings. Process on high until smooth. Pour vinegar mixture and broth over roast. Cover and cook on low setting for 6 to 8 hours, until roast is very tender. Shred beef with 2 forks; return to juices in slow cooker. Serve on tortillas with desired toppings. Serves 8.

Aimee Shugarman
Liberty Township, OH

My husband challenged me to create this spicy dish. Not only did I exceed his expectations, but I also ended up with a recipe that is so easy to prepare!

Chicken Taco Soup

1 onion, chopped
16-oz. can chili beans
15-oz. can black beans
15-oz. can corn
2 10-oz. cans diced tomatoes
   with green chiles
8-oz. can tomato sauce
12-oz. can beer or non-alcoholic
   beer
1-1/4 oz. pkg. taco seasoning mix
3 boneless, skinless chicken
   breasts
Garnish: shredded Cheddar
   cheese, crushed tortilla chips
Optional: sour cream

In a slow cooker, mix together onion, beans, corn, diced tomatoes with juice, tomato sauce and beer. Add seasoning mix; stir to blend. Lightly press chicken breasts into mixture in slow cooker until partially covered. Cover and cook on low setting for 5 hours. Remove chicken from slow cooker; shred and return to soup. Cover and cook for an additional 2 hours. Top servings of soup with cheese, crushed chips and sour cream, if desired. Serves 8.

33

Janet Allen
Hauser, ID

A spicy and flavorful soup...
serve this favorite with
bandannas for napkins and a
bottle of hot pepper sauce
for those who like it fiery!

Old-Fashioned Sage Dressing

2 c. onion, chopped
2 c. celery, chopped
1 c. butter
2 loaves white bread, torn
1-1/2 t. dried sage
1 t. dried thyme
1/2 t. dried marjoram
1 t. poultry seasoning
1-1/2 t. salt
1/2 t. pepper
14-1/2 oz. can chicken broth
2 eggs, beaten

In a skillet, sauté onion and celery in butter until fragrant; set aside. Place bread in a large bowl; add seasonings and mix well. Add onion mixture and enough broth to moisten bread; toss. Stir in eggs and mix well. Spoon into a slow cooker. Cover and cook on low setting for 6 to 8 hours, stirring occasionally and adding more broth as needed. Serves 10 to 12.

Gina Rongved-Van Wyk
Rapid City, SD

How clever! Make stuffing in your slow cooker to free up the oven for other dishes like roast turkey or baked yams.

No-Fuss Turkey Breast

4 to 5-lb. turkey breast
1.35-oz. pkg. onion soup mix
16-oz. can whole-berry cranberry
    sauce

Place turkey breast in a slow cooker.
In a bowl, combine soup mix and
cranberry sauce; spread over turkey.
Cover and cook on low setting for
6 to 8 hours. Serves 6.

35

Pat Wissler
Harrisburg, PA
With only three ingredients,
prep time is amazingly
fast...it's turkey and
cranberry sauce in one!
For a thinner sauce, just
drizzle in a little water.

Smoky Sausage & 2-Bean Soup

1 lb. smoked pork sausage, sliced
15-oz. can tomato sauce
2 14-1/2 oz. cans low-sodium
    beef broth
15-oz. can pinto beans, drained
    and rinsed
15-oz. can kidney beans, drained
    and rinsed
1/4 c. onion, chopped
1/4 c. celery, chopped
1/4 c. green pepper, chopped
1/4 c. red pepper, chopped
1 c. water
2 cubes beef bouillon
1/2 t. pepper
1/4 t. garlic salt
1/2 t. Italian seasoning
1 to 2 c. cooked rice

Combine all ingredients except rice
in a slow cooker. Cover and cook on
low setting for 6 to 8 hours. About
30 minutes before serving, stir in
rice. Cover and cook remaining
30 minutes. Makes 8 to 10 servings.

Rebecca Ross
Topeka, KS

I started making minestrone
and got carried away trying
to create a hearty soup for
a cold day! This is what
came out, and its flavor
just can't be beat.

Super-Easy Sausage Sandwiches

1-1/2 lbs. Italian pork sausage
   links
2 green peppers, sliced
1 onion, sliced
24-oz. can spaghetti sauce
pepper to taste
6 to 8 sandwich rolls, split

Place sausage links in a slow cooker.
Layer peppers and onion over links;
spoon sauce over all. Season with
pepper. Cover and cook on low
setting for 6 hours. Place sausages
in rolls and top with peppers,
onions and sauce from slow cooker.
Serves 6 to 8.

37

Beth Harman
Hegins, PA

Most of my family are
hunters, so I always use
homemade venison sausage,
but any sausage will do.
These sausages taste great
on a hearty sandwich roll.

Sausage-Stuffed Squash

14-oz. pkg. smoked pork sausage, diced
1/3 c. dark brown sugar, packed
1 T. butter-flavored sprinkles
1/4 t. dried sage
2 acorn squash, halved and seeded
1 c. water

In a bowl, mix together sausage, brown sugar, sprinkles and sage; toss to mix well. Fill squash halves heaping full with sausage mixture; wrap each stuffed half with aluminum foil. Pour water into a large slow cooker; place wrapped squash halves in slow cooker, stacking if necessary. Cover and cook on low setting for 6 to 8 hours. Makes 4 servings.

Angela Couillard
Lakeville, MN

Sweet, savory and oh-so tender! This tasty squash is a welcome addition to a holiday supper, or serve it as a simple weeknight meal.

Apple-Glazed Pork Roast

4-lb. pork loin roast
salt and pepper to taste
6 apples, cored and quartered
1/4 c. apple juice
3 T. brown sugar, packed
1 t. ground ginger

Season roast on all sides with salt and pepper. Place roast on a baking sheet and brown on both sides under a broiler. Arrange apples in a slow cooker; top with roast. In a bowl, whisk together juice, brown sugar and ginger; drizzle over roast. Cover and cook on high setting for 6 hours, or until roast is no longer pink in the center and apples are tender. Serves 8 to 10.

Rogene Rogers
Bemidji, MN

We love the combination of apples and pork. This smells so wonderful when it is cooking...like a perfect fall day. It's a family favorite!

Brunswick Stew

3-lb. boneless pork shoulder
   roast, quartered
3 redskin potatoes, diced
1 onion, chopped
28-oz. can crushed tomatoes
18-oz. bottle favorite barbecue
   sauce
14-oz. can chicken broth
9-oz. pkg. frozen baby lima
   beans, thawed
9-oz. pkg. frozen corn, thawed
6 T. brown sugar, packed
1 t. salt
Garnish: saltine crackers

Stir together all ingredients except crackers in a slow cooker. Cover and cook on high setting for 6 hours, or until pork and potatoes are tender. Remove pork with a slotted spoon; shred. Return pork to slow cooker; stir well. Ladle stew into bowls; serve with crackers. Serves 6.

Jennie Gist
Gooseberry Patch

This hearty stew is a fall and wintertime favorite around our house. I usually serve big bowls of it with a mug of hot cider.

Smoky Hobo Dinner

5 potatoes, peeled and quartered
1 head cabbage, coarsely chopped
16-oz. pkg. baby carrots
1 onion, thickly sliced
salt and pepper to taste
14-oz. pkg. smoked pork sausage,
   sliced into 2-inch pieces
1/2 c. water

Spray a slow cooker with non-stick
vegetable spray. Layer vegetables in
slow cooker in order listed,
sprinkling each layer with salt and
pepper. Place sausage on top of
vegetables in slow cooker; pour water
over all. Cover and cook on low
setting for 6 to 8 hours. Serves 6.

41

Julie Pak
Henryetta, OK
This recipe is one of my
special creations...my whole
family loves it, and I know
yours will too!

Warm & Wonderful Curried Vegetables

4 potatoes, peeled and diced
1 onion, chopped
1 red pepper, chopped
2 carrots, peeled and diced
2 to 3 tomatoes, chopped
6-oz. can tomato paste
3/4 c. water
2 T. curry powder
2 t. cumin seed
1/2 t. garlic powder
1/2 t. salt
3 c. cauliflower flowerets
10-oz. pkg. frozen peas, thawed

Place potatoes, onion, pepper, carrots and tomatoes in a slow cooker. Stir in tomato paste, water, curry powder, cumin seed, garlic powder and salt. Mix well and add cauliflower. Cook on low setting for 8 hours, or until vegetables are tender. Stir in peas just before serving. Serves 6 to 8.

Jill Burton
Gooseberry Patch

I first had this yummy dish at a potluck as a side...now I make it as a delicious meatless main served over some jasmine rice.

Chinese 5-Spice Chicken

1 stalk celery, sliced into 1-inch
    pieces
3 green onions, sliced into
    1-inch pieces
4 to 5-lb. roasting chicken
1 T. soy sauce
2 t. Chinese 5-spice powder

Place celery and onions inside
chicken. In a bowl, combine soy
sauce and spice powder to make
a paste; rub over chicken. Place
chicken in a large slow cooker,
on a rack, if desired. Cover and
cook on low setting for 6 to 7 hours,
until chicken is tender and juices
run clear when pierced. Discard
vegetables inside chicken; carve to
serve. Serves 4.

43

Regina Wickline
Pebble Beach, CA
The taste of Chinese 5-spice
powder is really unique and
gives this chicken great
flavor. Serve with steamed
vegetables and rice.

Winter Barbecued Chicken

1-1/2 t. paprika
1/2 t. garlic powder
2 t. salt
1/2 t. pepper
3 lbs. chicken
1/2 c. cola
1/3 c. catsup
1/4 c. light brown sugar, packed
2 T. cider vinegar
Optional: 2 T. bourbon
1 lemon, sliced

In a bowl, stir together seasonings. Place chicken pieces in a slow cooker and sprinkle with seasoning mixture; toss to coat. In a separate bowl, whisk together remaining ingredients except lemon. Pour cola mixture over chicken; place lemon slices on top. Cover and cook on low setting for 6 to 7 hours, until chicken juices run clear. Remove chicken to a serving platter and discard lemon. Spoon sauce in slow cooker over chicken. Serves 6 to 8.

Mia Rossi
Charlotte, NC

Can't wait for barbecued chicken? You don't have to with this simple slow-cooker recipe. Now you can enjoy mouthwatering barbecued chicken any time of year!

Teriyaki Pork Roast

3/4 c. apple juice
2 T. sugar
2 T. soy sauce
1 T. cider vinegar
1 t. ground ginger
1/4 t. garlic powder
1/8 t. pepper
2 to 3-lb. boneless center-cut
   rolled pork roast
1-1/2 T. cornstarch
3 T. cold water
Garnish: sliced green onions

Combine juice, sugar, soy sauce, vinegar and seasonings in a slow cooker; mix well. Add roast, turning to coat; place roast fat-side up. Cover and cook on low setting for 7 to 8 hours. Strain liquid into a small saucepan; bring to a boil. Mix together cornstarch and water in a small bowl; add to boiling liquid. Cook until thickened. Slice roast, serving gravy over top; sprinkle with green onions. Serves 4 to 6.

45

Jodi Erdmann
Watertown, WI

For a tasty meal idea, shred the cooked pork, stir it into the liquids in the slow cooker, then spoon the pork mixture onto toasted buns for teriyaki sandwiches.

Maple Praline Chicken

6 boneless, skinless chicken
   breasts
2 T. Cajun seasoning
1/4 c. butter, melted
1/2 c. maple syrup
2 T. brown sugar, packed
1 c. chopped pecans
6-oz. pkg. long-grain and wild
   rice, cooked

Sprinkle chicken with Cajun
seasoning. In a skillet over medium-
high heat, cook chicken in butter
until golden. Arrange chicken in a
slow cooker. In a bowl, mix together
syrup, brown sugar and pecans;
spoon over chicken. Cover and cook
on low setting for 6 to 8 hours. Serve
with cooked rice. Serves 6.

Jill Valentine
Jackson, TN

I have a neighbor who
bottles his own maple syrup,
and it really makes this
dish taste wonderful...
so sweet and flavorful!

Dilly Beet Soup

3 lbs. beets, peeled and
   quartered
1 onion, quartered
3-1/4 c. chicken broth
3-1/4 c. water
1-1/2 t. salt
1 T. lemon juice
2 T. fresh dill, chopped
1/4 t. pepper
Optional: 1 hard-boiled egg,
   peeled and sliced

Combine beets, onion, broth, water
and salt in a slow cooker. Cover and
cook on low setting for 8 hours.
Using a blender, purée soup in
batches, returning to slow cooker
when smooth. Stir in lemon juice,
dill and pepper. Garnish servings
with additional fresh dill and egg
slices, if desired. Serves 6.

47

Virginia Watson
Scranton, PA

This old-fashioned classic
is perfect for using up all
the beets from my garden. My
husband loves the fresh
dill flavor and vibrant
color of this soup.

Zippy Chile Verde

3 T. olive oil
1/2 c. onion, chopped
2 cloves garlic, minced
3-lb. boneless pork shoulder,
  cubed
5 7-oz. cans green salsa
4-oz. can diced jalapeño peppers
14-1/2 oz. can diced tomatoes

Heat oil in a large skillet over
medium heat. Add onion and garlic
to oil; cook and stir until fragrant,
about 2 minutes. Add pork to skillet;
cook until browned on all sides.
Transfer pork mixture to a slow
cooker; stir in salsa, jalapeño peppers
and tomatoes with juice. Cover and
cook on high setting for 3 hours.
Turn to low setting; cover and cook
for 4 to 5 more hours. Serves 8.

Vickie
This tangy pork dish is
perfect served over steamed
rice and black beans or
wrapped up in a tortilla
with a little Pepper Jack
or Mexican-blend cheese.

Hawaiian Ham Sammies

2 lbs. cooked ham, thinly sliced
1/4 c. onion, chopped
1 c. catsup
1/2 c. water
1/2 c. vinegar
1/4 c. mustard
1/4 c. plus 2 T. brown sugar,
  packed
2 T. Worcestershire sauce
8 Kaiser rolls, split
15-1/4 oz. can pineapple slices,
  drained

49

Combine all ingredients except rolls and pineapple in a slow cooker. Cover and cook on low setting for 6 to 8 hours. Serve ham mixture on split rolls, topped with pineapple slices. Serves 8.

Satoko Harjo
Edmonds, WA

My friends and I get together every six to eight weeks and exchange frozen dinners. Hawaiian Ham Sammies is the most-requested main dish!

Beans Southwestern Style

6 c. low-sodium chicken broth
1 onion, chopped
2 T. diced green chiles
1 carrot, peeled and chopped
1 stalk celery, chopped
14-1/2 oz. can diced tomatoes
4 cloves garlic, finely chopped
1 T. ground cumin
3 c. dried pinto beans
1 c. dried black beans
1-1/2 lb. pork shoulder roast
Garnish: chopped fresh cilantro,
  salsa verde
Optional: sour cream

Combine broth, vegetables, tomatoes
with juice, garlic and cumin in a slow
cooker. Add beans and pork to broth
mixture. Cover and cook on low
setting for 8 hours, until beans are
tender and pork pulls apart easily.
Remove pork from slow cooker and
shred; set aside. Using a blender or
immersion blender, purée about half
of the beans and liquid mixture.
Spoon pork back into slow cooker;
mix well. Top servings with cilantro,
salsa and sour cream, if desired.
Serves 8 to 10.

Teresa Grimsley
Alamosa, CO

I've developed this recipe
over time, and it is
absolutely the best bean
recipe I've ever had! It's
perfect with a big piece of
cornbread after a chilly day
of snowshoeing.

Spaghetti Sauce with Italian Sausage

1 T. olive oil
6 Italian pork sausage links
1 c. green pepper, chopped
1 onion, chopped
2 cloves garlic, sliced
28-oz. can crushed tomatoes
2 8-oz. cans tomato sauce
6-oz. can tomato paste
1/4 c. sugar
1 T. dried basil
1 T. dried oregano
1 T. Italian seasoning
salt and pepper to taste
cooked ziti pasta

Heat oil in a skillet over medium heat. Brown sausages with green pepper, onion and garlic. Add tomatoes with juice and remaining ingredients except pasta to a slow cooker; mix well. Spoon sausage mixture into tomato mixture in slow cooker. Cover and cook on low setting for 6 hours. Serve sausages and sauce over cooked pasta. Serves 8 to 10.

Amy Fehlberg
Allison, IA

This recipe was given to me by my best friend of 20 years. She's not a great cook, but this meal makes up for all the others... it's delicious!

Irish Corned Beef Dinner

3-lb. corned beef brisket
4 to 6 potatoes, quartered
1 lb. carrots, peeled, halved and
    cut into sticks
1 head cabbage, cut into wedges
2 onions, quartered
12-oz. can beer or non-alcoholic
    beer
1 bay leaf
2 to 3 c. water

Place brisket in a slow cooker.
Arrange vegetables around brisket;
add beer, bay leaf and enough water
to cover. Cover and cook on low
setting for 7 to 8 hours. Discard bay
leaf. To serve, arrange vegetables on
a large serving platter. Slice brisket
and arrange over vegetables. Makes
6 servings.

Lisanne Miller
Canton, MS

Serve with rye bread
and spicy mustard for
a tasty meal!

Paprika Beef & Noodles

1-3/4 c. water, divided
2 lbs. stew beef cubes
1 c. onion, sliced
1 clove garlic, diced
3/4 c. catsup
2 T. Worcestershire sauce
1 T. brown sugar, packed
2 t. salt
2 t. paprika
1/8 t. dry mustard
1/8 t. cayenne pepper
2 T. all-purpose flour
cooked egg noodles

53

In a slow cooker, combine 1-1/2 cups water and remaining ingredients except flour and noodles; mix well. Cover and cook on low setting for 6 to 8 hours. In a cup, stir together remaining water and flour. Drizzle into beef mixture; stir. Cook, uncovered, until thickened. Serve beef mixture over noodles.
Serves 6 to 8.

Teresa Pearman
Marshall, NC

My mom always made this delicious meal during the cold winter months...it always warms you up.

Crockery Chicken Curry

1-1/2 lbs. boneless, skinless
   chicken thighs, cubed
2 carrots, peeled and sliced
1 onion, thinly sliced
2 T. cornstarch
4 t. curry powder
3/4 t. turmeric
salt and pepper to taste
1/2 head cauliflower, cut into
   flowerets
2 cloves garlic, minced
1/3 c. water
1-1/4 c. plain non-fat yogurt
1/4 c. fresh cilantro, chopped

Combine chicken, carrots and onion
in a slow cooker. In a small bowl, stir
together cornstarch and seasonings.
Sprinkle cornstarch mixture over
chicken mixture; toss to coat well.
Add cauliflower, garlic and water to
slow cooker. Cover and cook on low
setting for 8 hours. Spoon one cup
of juice from slow cooker into a
bowl; stir in yogurt and cilantro.
Stir yogurt mixture back into slow
cooker. Serves 6.

Gracie Smith
Vancouver, British Columbia

This fragrant dish is
perfect after a long, chilly
day at work. Serve over
cooked jasmine rice or
fluffy quinoa.

Orange & Ginger Beef Short Ribs

1/3 c. soy sauce
3 T. brown sugar, packed
3 T. white vinegar
2 cloves garlic, minced
1/2 t. chili powder
1 T. fresh ginger, peeled and
   minced
3 lbs. boneless beef short ribs
1/3 c. orange marmalade

In a large plastic zipping bag,
combine all ingredients except ribs
and marmalade. Add ribs to bag;
turn to coat well. Refrigerate at least
2 hours to overnight. Drain ribs,
reserving marinade. Place ribs in a
slow cooker. Add marmalade to
reserved marinade; mix well and
pour over ribs. Cover and cook on
low setting for 6 to 8 hours. Serves 6.

55

Lee Beedle
Martinsburg, WV
I always thought beef ribs
and marmalade would go
together perfectly in the
slow cooker. When I tried
this recipe, I knew right
away it was a keeper.

Savory Slow-Cooked Cornish Hens

4 20-oz. Cornish game hens,
   thawed
2 T. oil
4 redskin potatoes, sliced
   1/8-inch thick
4 slices bacon, cut into 1-inch
   pieces
lemon-pepper seasoning and
   garlic powder to taste
Garnish: minced fresh parsley

Brown hens in oil in a large skillet
over medium heat until golden on
all sides. Layer potato slices in a
large slow cooker; arrange hens on
potatoes. Top with bacon. Sprinkle
with seasonings. Cover and cook on
low setting for 6 to 8 hours, until
juices run clear and potatoes are
tender. Garnish with parsley.
Serves 4.

Kendall Hale
Lynn, MA

These pretty little hens
are sure to impress your
family & friends. My roomy
6-quart slow cooker is
perfect for this recipe.

Roast Turkey & Cranberry Dressing

8-oz. pkg. stuffing mix
1/2 c. hot water
2 T. butter, softened
1 onion, chopped
1/2 c. celery, chopped
1/4 c. sweetened dried
   cranberries
3-lb. boneless turkey breast
1/4 t. dried basil
1/2 t. salt
1/2 t. pepper

Place stuffing mix in a slow cooker. Add water, butter, onion, celery and cranberries; mix well. Sprinkle turkey with seasonings; place on top of stuffing mixture. Cover and cook on low setting for 6 to 7 hours. Remove turkey to a cutting board; stir stuffing until thoroughly mixed. Let turkey and stuffing stand for 5 minutes. Spoon stuffing onto a platter and top with sliced turkey. Serves 4 to 6.

57

Barbara Shultis
South Egremont, MA

This recipe is one of the easiest I know of...your slow cooker does all the work! It has all the flavors of a scrumptious Thanksgiving meal, but with less work.

Perfectly Peachy Cake

3/4 c. biscuit baking mix
1/2 c. brown sugar, packed
1/3 c. sugar
2 eggs, beaten
2 t. vanilla extract
1/2 c. evaporated milk
2 t. butter, melted
3 peaches, peeled, pitted and
    mashed
3/4 t. cinnamon
Garnish: vanilla ice cream

In a large bowl, combine baking mix
and sugars. Stir in eggs and vanilla
until blended. Mix in milk and
butter. Fold in peaches and
cinnamon until well mixed. Spoon
mixture into a lightly greased slow
cooker. Cover and cook on low
setting for 6 to 8 hours. Serve warm,
topped with a scoop of ice cream.
Serves 4 to 6.

Sue Learned
Wilton, CA

This cake is just right
to make in the summertime
because you don't have to
turn on your oven and
heat up the kitchen.

Crockery Apple Pie

8 tart apples, peeled, cored
    and sliced
2 t. cinnamon
1/4 t. allspice
1/4 t. nutmeg
3/4 c. milk
2 T. butter, softened
3/4 c. sugar
2 eggs, beaten
1 t. vanilla extract
1-1/2 c. biscuit baking mix,
    divided
1/3 c. brown sugar, packed
3 T. chilled butter

In a large bowl, toss apples with spices. Spoon apple mixture into a lightly greased slow cooker. In a separate bowl, combine milk, softened butter, sugar, eggs, vanilla and 1/2 cup baking mix; stir until well mixed. Spoon batter over apples. Place remaining baking mix and brown sugar in a small bowl. Cut in chilled butter until coarse crumbs form. Sprinkle over batter in slow cooker. Cover and cook on low setting for 6 to 7 hours.
Serves 10 to 12.

59

Gretchen Hickman
Galva, IL

received this recipe
from my great-aunt who
owned an orchard. This
smells heavenly when it's
cooking, and it's perfect
served with a big scoop of
vanilla bean ice cream.

Chunky Applesauce

10 apples, peeled, cored
  and cubed
1/2 c. water
3/4 c. sugar
Optional: 1 t. cinnamon

Combine all ingredients in a slow
cooker; toss to mix. Cover and cook
on low setting for 8 to 10 hours.
Serve warm or keep refrigerated
in a covered container. Makes 6 to
8 servings.

Lisa Ann Panzino-DiNunzio
Vineland, NJ

This applesauce is a must
alongside pork dishes! Fuji,
Gala and Golden Delicious
apples are all excellent
in this recipe.

Barbecued Beer Chicken

3 to 4-lb. roasting chicken
1/4 c. barbecue seasoning
12-oz. bottle regular or non-
    alcoholic beer

Spray a large slow cooker with
non-stick vegetable spray. Carefully
loosen skin from chicken. Rub
seasoning generously under and on
top of skin. Place chicken in a slow
cooker; pour beer over chicken.
Cover and cook on low setting for
8 hours. Serves 6.

Kristy Markners
Fort Mill, SC
This chicken is very moist
and delicious. My three-year-
old son gets so excited when
we buy whole chickens at
the grocery store...he says
"Cock-a-doodle-zoo!"
all the way home!

Susan's Slow-Cookin' Ribs

1 T. onion powder
1 t. red pepper flakes
1/2 t. dry mustard
1/2 t. garlic powder
1/2 t. allspice
1/2 t. cinnamon
3 lbs. boneless pork ribs, sliced
    into serving-size pieces
1 onion, sliced and divided
1/2 c. water
2 c. hickory-flavored barbecue
    sauce

Combine seasonings in a cup; mix well and rub over ribs. Arrange one-third of ribs in a slow cooker. Place one-third of onion slices over top; repeat layering 2 more times, ending with onion. Pour water over all. Cover and cook on low setting for 8 to 10 hours. Drain and discard liquid from slow cooker. Pour barbecue sauce over ribs. Cover and cook on low setting for an additional one to 2 hours. Serves 6 to 8.

Susan Ice
Snohomish, WA
These ribs melt in your mouth! I always make a double batch and freeze half. They can be eaten as is, or shredded and used for sandwiches.

Chicken Tortilla Soup

3 boneless, skinless chicken
   breasts
2 15-oz. cans black beans
15-oz. can corn, drained
2 14-1/2 oz. cans diced tomatoes
   with green chiles
1 c. salsa
14-1/2 oz. can tomato sauce
Garnish: shredded Pepper Jack
   cheese, sour cream, crushed
   tortilla chips

Add all ingredients except garnish in
order listed to a slow cooker. Cover
and cook on low setting for 9 hours.
Remove chicken from soup; shred
and return to soup. Top servings with
cheese, a dollop of sour cream and
crushed chips. Serves 4 to 6.

Lanay McCord
Long Beach, CA

This recipe was given to
me by a friend many years
ago...I was looking for
something quick & easy yet
hearty. I've passed it on
to my daughter, and her
family loves it!

Old-Fashioned Pork & Sauerkraut

2 32-oz. pkgs. sauerkraut
2 c. water
salt and pepper to taste
3-lb. boneless pork tenderloin

Place sauerkraut with juice in a
slow cooker. Drizzle water over
sauerkraut; season with salt and
pepper. Place pork on top of
sauerkraut mixture; season with salt
and pepper again, if preferred. Cover
and cook on low setting for 8 to
10 hours, until pork is very tender.
Serves 6 to 8.

Sharon Golden
Shamokin, PA
This recipe was handed down
to me by my mother-in-law
Doris. We serve it with
mashed potatoes...a wonderful
tradition in our small town.

Savory Slow-Cooked Pork Loin

2-lb. pork loin, quartered
1.2-oz. pkg. brown gravy mix
1 c. water
1 c. apple juice
1/2 c. applesauce
2 t. Worcestershire sauce
1 stalk celery, sliced into
   1/2-inch pieces
1 onion, chopped
1-1/2 t. seasoned salt
1/2 t. pepper
Optional: 1 T. cornstarch,
   1 T. water

Place pork in a slow cooker. In a
bowl, combine gravy mix and
water; stir until dissolved. Add
remaining ingredients except
optional cornstarch and water to
gravy mixture; mix well. Spoon gravy
mixture over pork. Cover and cook
on low setting for 8 hours, or until
meat is very tender. If liquid in
slow cooker needs to be thickened,
whisk together cornstarch and
one tablespoon water in a cup. Stir
into slow cooker during the last
30 minutes of cooking. Serves 4 to 6.

Kathleen Hendrick
Alexandria, KY

This is one of my family's
favorite recipes...the pork
is always tender and
delicious. We like to serve
this pork with mashed
potatoes and peas.

Italian Wedding Soup

25 frozen cooked Italian
   meatballs
6 c. chicken broth
1 c. boneless, skinless chicken
   breast, chopped
1/2 c. carrot, peeled and diced
1/2 c. celery, diced
1 bunch spinach, torn
garlic salt to taste
1/4 c. grated Parmesan-Romano
   cheese
1/4 c. ditalini pasta, uncooked
Garnish: grated Parmesan-
   Romano cheese

Combine all ingredients except pasta
and garnish in a slow cooker. Cover
and cook on low setting for 8 hours.
About 20 minutes before serving,
cook pasta according to package
directions; drain and stir into slow
cooker. Sprinkle servings with a little
more cheese. Serves 6 to 8.

LuAnn Tracy
Aliquippa, PA
I got this wonderful recipe
from my sister's daughter-
in-law...serve with a tangy
salad and bread sticks for
a simple meal.

Herb Garden Chicken

4 to 6 boneless, skinless chicken breasts
2 tomatoes, chopped
1 onion, chopped
2 cloves garlic, chopped
2/3 c. chicken broth
1 bay leaf
1 t. dried thyme
1-1/2 t. salt
1 t. pepper, or more to taste
2 c. broccoli flowerets
Optional: 2 to 3 T. all-purpose flour
cooked rice

67

Place chicken in a slow cooker; top with tomatoes, onion and garlic. In a bowl, combine broth and seasonings; pour over chicken mixture. Cover and cook on low setting for 8 hours. Add broccoli; cook for one additional hour, or until chicken juices run clear and broccoli is tender. Juices in slow cooker may be thickened with flour, if desired. Discard bay leaf; serve chicken and vegetables over cooked rice. Makes 4 to 6 servings.

Julie Neff
Citrus Springs, FL
This is the chicken dish my husband asks for most often. I'm happy to oblige because it's so tasty and so easy to put together.

Sweet & Spicy Country-Style Ribs

2 to 3 lbs. bone-in country-style
    pork ribs, sliced into serving-
    size pieces
1 onion, sliced
salt and pepper to taste
18-oz. bottle favorite barbecue
    sauce
1/2 c. maple syrup
1/4 c. spicy brown mustard

Place ribs in a slow cooker that has
been sprayed with non-stick vegetable
spray. Place onion on top of ribs;
sprinkle with salt and pepper. In a
bowl, mix together remaining
ingredients; pour over all. Cover and
cook on low setting for 8 to
10 hours. Makes 4 to 6 servings.

Kandy Bingham
Green River, WY

My husband Randy and I made
up this recipe for our slow
cooker because we love
barbecued ribs. Why go for
take-out when you can make
these scrumptious ribs right
in your own kitchen?

Creole Shrimp & Sausage

1 onion, chopped
1 green pepper, chopped
2 stalks celery, sliced
2 carrots, peeled and diced
4 cloves garlic, minced
14-1/2 oz. can diced tomatoes
3/4 c. chicken broth
2 t. Creole seasoning
3 andouille pork sausage links,
   cut into 1/2-inch pieces
10-oz. pkg. frozen corn, thawed
1 T. tomato paste
1 lb. large shrimp, peeled and
   cleaned
cooked rice

In a large bowl, combine onion, pepper, celery, carrots, garlic, tomatoes with juice, broth and seasoning. Mix well; stir in sausage and corn. Add mixture to a lightly greased slow cooker. Cover and cook on low setting for 8 hours. Stir in tomato paste and shrimp. Cover and cook for 7 to 10 more minutes, until shrimp is cooked. Spoon over rice to serve. Serves 6.

69

Kerry Mayer
Dunham Springs, LA

We used to live on the Gulf, and I would watch the shrimping boats come in and go out all the time. I'd be sure to pick up some fresh shrimp to make this delectable dish too!

Slow-Cooked Veggie-Beef Soup

1 to 1-1/2 lbs. stew beef cubes
46-oz. can cocktail vegetable
   juice
2 c. water
5 cubes beef bouillon
1/2 onion, chopped
2 to 3 potatoes, peeled and cubed
3 c. cabbage, shredded
16-oz. pkg. frozen mixed
   vegetables

Place all ingredients in a slow cooker.
Cover and cook on low setting for
9 hours, or until all ingredients are
tender. Makes 10 to 12 servings.

Pat Beach
Fisherville, KY

For someone who couldn't even
boil water when she got
married, my daughter Toni is
a fabulous cook! She says all
it takes to be a great cook
is a good, full-flavored
recipe like this one.

Shredded Buffalo Chicken Sliders

4 boneless, skinless chicken
   breasts
1/4 c. cayenne hot pepper sauce
2/3 c. water
16 dinner rolls, split
1 c. blue cheese salad dressing
Garnish: celery sticks

Place chicken breasts in a lightly greased slow cooker. In a bowl, stir together hot sauce and water; drizzle over chicken. Cover and cook on low setting for 8 hours. Remove chicken and shred with 2 forks; return to sauce in slow cooker. To serve, place shredded chicken on bottom halves of rolls; evenly top with dressing. Replace tops of rolls. Serve with celery sticks. Serves 8.

71

Nola Coons
Gooseberry Patch

These scrumptious mini sandwiches are always a hit at parties or get-togethers.

French Dips on a Budget

3 to 4-lb. beef rump roast
1/2 c. soy sauce
1.35-oz. pkg. onion soup mix
salt and pepper to taste
3 to 4 c. water
4 to 6 sandwich rolls, split

Place roast in a slow cooker. Drizzle with soy sauce; sprinkle with soup mix, salt and pepper. Add enough water to cover roast. Cover and cook on low setting for 10 hours, or until beef is very tender. Remove beef from slow cooker and slice or shred. To serve, place beef on rolls for sandwiches; serve with juices from slow cooker for dipping.
Serves 4 to 6.

Cheryl Sullivan
Winfield, IA

One day, my mother and I were craving a French dip sandwich, so we put our heads together and came up with this tasty recipe.

Dad's Famous Minestrone

4 carrots, peeled and sliced
1 c. celery, chopped
1 c. onion, chopped
5 to 6 red potatoes, diced
3 zucchini, sliced
14-1/2 oz. can diced tomatoes
15-oz. can cut green beans
8 cloves garlic, chopped
3 T. olive oil
1-1/2 t. dried basil
1 t. dried rosemary
2 T. dried parsley
1/2 t. sea salt
1/2 t. pepper
3 14-oz. cans chicken broth
12-oz. bottle cocktail vegetable
    juice
1 bunch escarole, chopped
15-oz. can garbanzo beans
15-oz. can cannellini beans
8-oz. pkg. ditalini pasta,
    uncooked
Garnish: grated Parmesan cheese

To a slow cooker, add all ingredients
in order listed except beans, pasta
and garnish. Cover and cook on low
setting for 8 hours. After 8 hours,
stir in beans and pasta; cook for
one more hour. Top servings with
cheese. Serves 8 to 10.

73

Glenn Stracqualursi
Lakeland, FL

My dad made this tasty
soup for years at his
park's fundraiser events
and never had any left by
the end...this one's
in honor of my dad.

Apple Butter BBQ Spareribs

4 lbs. pork spareribs
salt and pepper to taste
16-oz. jar apple butter
18-oz. bottle barbecue sauce
1 onion, quartered

Sprinkle ribs with salt and pepper.
Place ribs on rimmed baking sheets.
Bake at 350 degrees for 30 minutes;
drain. Meanwhile, blend together
apple butter and barbecue sauce in
a bowl; set aside. Slice ribs into
serving-size pieces and place in a
slow cooker. Top with onion; drizzle
sauce mixture over all. Cover and
cook on low setting for 8 hours.
Makes 4 to 6 servings.

Catherine Rivard
Moline, IL

Theses ribs taste amazing...
my family absolutely loves
them! For a change, try this
same recipe using a pork or
beef roast and add apricot
preserves in place of the
apple butter.

Beef & Butternut Stew

2 t. dried thyme
2 t. salt
3/4 t. pepper
5 T. cornstarch
1-1/2 lb. beef round roast, cubed
1 bulb fennel, sliced
3/4 lb. redskin potatoes,
   quartered
28-oz. can whole tomatoes,
   drained and tomatoes halved
1 butternut squash, peeled,
   seeded and cubed
1 t. olive oil

75

Combine seasonings in a bowl;
reserve one teaspoon seasoning
mixture. Combine cornstarch with
remaining seasoning mixture. Toss
beef, fennel and potatoes in
cornstarch mixture until well coated.
Transfer beef mixture to a slow
cooker; spoon tomatoes over top. In
a separate bowl, toss squash with oil
and reserved spice mixture. Layer
squash on top of tomatoes. Cover
and cook on low setting for 8 hours.
Serves 8 to 10.

JoAnn

I always grow some butternut
squash in my garden every
year. I love to give them
away to friends &
neighbors...but I really
love making this delicious
stew with them!

Pork & Pinto Stew

16-oz. pkg. dried pinto beans
3-lb. boneless pork loin roast
7 c. water
4-oz. can chopped green chiles
1/2 c. onion, chopped
2 cloves garlic, minced
2 T. chili powder
1 T. ground cumin
1 T. salt
1 t. dried oregano
Garnish: corn chips, sour cream,
    shredded Cheddar cheese,
    chopped tomatoes, shredded
    lettuce

Cover beans with water in a large soup pot; soak overnight. Drain. Add beans and remaining ingredients except garnish to a slow cooker. Cover and cook on low setting for 9 hours; remove pork from slow cooker. Shred pork and return to slow cooker. Cook, uncovered, for 30 minutes, or until thickened. Serve over corn chips, garnished as desired. Serves 10.

Jason Keller
Carrollton, GA
This is one of our family's favorite dinners. We like to serve this thick & chunky stew over some corn chips or tortilla chips for a twist!

Unstuffed Cabbage

1 lb. ground beef
1/2 c. onion, chopped
1/2 c. celery, sliced
3 cloves garlic, finely chopped
1 head cabbage, chopped
28-oz. can stewed tomatoes
6-oz. can tomato paste
1 t. sugar
1-1/2 t. dried parsley
1 t. dried oregano
1/4 t. pepper
Optional: hot pepper sauce
    to taste
Garnish: shredded Cheddar
    cheese

In a large skillet over medium heat, cook beef, onion, celery and garlic until beef is no longer pink. Drain; transfer to a lightly greased slow cooker. Top with cabbage. In a large bowl, combine tomatoes with juice and tomato paste. Break up tomatoes with a potato masher. Stir in sugar, seasonings and hot sauce, if using. Spoon over cabbage. Cover and cook on low setting for 8 to 10 hours. Top servings with cheese. Serves 4 to 6.

Diane Cohen
Breinigsville, PA
Originally this recipe was for the stovetop, but I adapted it for the slow cooker. It's yummy served over mashed potatoes!

77

French Onion Beef Stew

14-1/2 oz. can chicken broth
1 c. apple juice
4 carrots, peeled and sliced
2 onions, thinly sliced
8 sprigs fresh thyme
1-1/2 lbs. stew beef cubes
salt and pepper to taste
3 T. all-purpose flour
4 thick slices French bread
1 c. Gruyère cheese, shredded

Combine broth, juice, carrots, onions and thyme in a slow cooker. Sprinkle beef with salt, pepper and flour; toss to coat well. Add beef to slow cooker; mix well. Cover and cook on low setting for 8 hours. Just before serving, place bread slices on a baking sheet; sprinkle evenly with cheese. Broil for one to 2 minutes, until cheese is melted and golden. Spoon stew into bowls; top each with a cheese toast. Serves 4.

Connie Hilty
Pearland, TX

This scrumptious soup is a breeze to toss together for a simple Sunday meal...looks pretty too!

Italian Meatball Subs

1 lb. ground beef
1 c. Italian-seasoned dry
   bread crumbs
1/2 c. grated Parmesan cheese
1 T. fresh parsley, minced
1 clove garlic, minced
1/2 c. milk
1 egg
1-1/2 t. salt
1/2 t. pepper
8 sub buns, split
Garnish: shredded mozzarella
   cheese

Combine all ingredients except buns
and mozzarella in a large bowl; mix
well. Form into 2-inch balls; place in
slow cooker. Spoon Sauce over top.
Cover and cook on low setting for
8 to 10 hours. Place 3 to 4 meatballs
on each bun; top with sauce and
mozzarella. Makes 8 sandwiches.

Sauce:

28-oz. can tomato purée
28-oz. can Italian-style crushed
   tomatoes
1/2 c. grated Parmesan cheese
2 1-1/2 oz. pkgs. spaghetti sauce
   mix
salt and pepper to taste

Mix all ingredients in a saucepan over
medium heat; simmer.

Clydia Mims
Effingham, SC

This recipe is so good!
I like to make a double batch
and freeze half for another
meal...the meatballs are
good over pasta too!

79

Too-Easy Rotisserie Chicken

2 t. kosher salt
1 t. paprika
1 t. onion powder
1 t. Italian seasoning
1/2 t. dried thyme
1/2 t. cayenne pepper
1/2 t. pepper
1/8 t. chili powder
4 to 5-lb. roasting chicken
4 cloves garlic
1 onion, quartered

Combine spices in a bowl. Rub spice mixture over all sides of chicken. Place chicken, breast-side down, in a slow cooker. Put garlic and onions inside chicken cavity. Cover and cook on low setting for 8 to 10 hours, until juices run clear. Serves 4 to 6.

Sandra Sullivan
Aurora, CO
Like store-bought rotisserie chicken...but better! It's moister and has much less fat. In short, this chicken is fantastic.

No-Peek Stew

6 carrots, peeled and thickly
 sliced
3 potatoes, peeled and cubed
1 onion, sliced
3 stalks celery, sliced into 1-inch
 pieces
2 lbs. stew beef cubes
1/4 c. all-purpose flour
1 T. sugar
1 T. salt
1/4 t. pepper
14-oz. can tomato sauce

Arrange vegetables in a slow cooker;
top with beef. In a bowl, blend flour,
sugar, salt and pepper; sprinkle over
beef. Pour tomato sauce over all;
cover and cook on low setting for 8 to
9 hours. Makes 4 to 6 servings.

81

Lisa Hoag
North Aurora, IL

My mother used to bake this
in the oven for Sunday
dinner. By mid-day it would
smell so good and we would
start asking, "Is it done
yet? Can we peek?"

Easy Kielbasa Dinner

10 to 12 new redskin potatoes
16-oz. pkg. sauerkraut
1/4 c. water
1 t. caraway seed
1 T. light brown sugar, packed
16-oz. Kielbasa sausage ring,
   cut into 2-inch pieces

If desired, pare a strip around the middle of each potato. Arrange potatoes in a slow cooker. Place undrained sauerkraut on top of potatoes; rinse sauerkraut package with a little water and pour into slow cooker. Sprinkle caraway seed and brown sugar over sauerkraut; arrange Kielbasa pieces over all. Cover and cook on low setting for 8 to 10 hours. Serves 4.

Denny Shaw
Drexel Hill, PA
There's nothing better than opening the door after a long day, smelling the delicious aroma and knowing my dinner is ready!

Bean & Sausage Soup

48-oz. container chicken broth
15-oz. can black beans, drained
15-oz. can pinto beans
15-oz. can black-eyed peas
16-oz. smoked pork sausage ring,
   cut into 8 sections
1 onion, chopped
1 red pepper, chopped
1 clove garlic, chopped
2 T. sugar
salt and pepper to taste
9-oz. pkg. frozen corn

In a slow cooker, combine broth, sausage, black beans and undrained pinto beans and black-eyed peas. Add remaining ingredients except corn. Cover and cook on low setting for 8 hours. Turn to high setting and stir in corn; cover and cook one hour longer. Serves 4 to 6.

83

**Mary Paige Boyce
Columbia, SC**

I put this scrumptious soup in the slow cooker in the morning, and when I get home, I have a great nutritious supper. I like to serve bowls of it with a big square of corn bread.

Soupe au Pistou

4 carrots, peeled and chopped
3 potatoes, peeled and chopped
2 onions, chopped
14-1/2 oz. can diced tomatoes
8 c. vegetable broth
salt and pepper to taste
15-oz. can cannellini beans,
   drained and rinsed
1 c. elbow macaroni, uncooked
1/2 c. basil pesto sauce

Combine vegetables and broth in a slow cooker; season with salt and pepper. Cover and cook on low setting for 8 hours, or until vegetables are tender. Stir in beans and macaroni. Cover and cook until macaroni is tender, about 30 minutes. Top servings with a tablespoon of pesto. Serves 8.

Nancy Wise
Little Rock, AR

This is a very old-fashioned dish with an amazing flavor. It's a savory vegetable soup with a delicious dollop of pesto in it to add loads of taste.

Zesty Italian Pot Roast

4 potatoes, peeled and quartered
2 c. baby carrots
1 stalk celery, cut into 1-inch
    slices
2-1/2 lb. boneless beef chuck
    roast
1/2 t. pepper
14-1/2 oz. diced tomatoes with
    basil, garlic and oregano
1/4 c. water
Optional: 1/4 c. all-purpose
    flour, 1/2 c. cold water

Arrange vegetables in a slow cooker.
Top with roast; sprinkle with pepper.
In a bowl, mix undrained tomatoes
and water; pour over roast. Cover
and cook on low setting for 8 to 10
hours. Serve roast surrounded with
vegetables; transfer drippings to a
gravy boat. If a thicker gravy is
desired, remove roast from slow
cooker; keep warm. Mix flour and
cold water; stir into drippings in
slow cooker. Turn heat to high
setting; cook until mixture boils
and thickens, about 10 minutes.
Serves 4 to 6.

Laura Dossantos
Rutherfordton, NC
Just add a loaf of warm
bread...dinner is ready!

Very Veggie Chili

1 T. olive oil
2 c. carrots, peeled and diced
1 c. celery, diced
1 onion, diced
16-oz. pkg. sliced mushrooms
2 zucchini, chopped
2 yellow squash, chopped
1 T. chili powder
1 t. dried basil
1 t. pepper
4 8-oz. cans tomato sauce
1 c. vegetable broth
2 14-1/2 oz. cans diced tomatoes
2 15-oz. cans black beans,
    drained and rinsed
2 15-oz. cans dark red kidney
    beans, drained and rinsed
Optional: 1 c. frozen corn,
    2 c. kale or spinach

Heat oil in a large skillet over medium heat. Sauté carrots, celery and onion in oil for 5 minutes. Stir in mushrooms, zucchini and squash; sauté for 3 minutes. Sprinkle with seasonings; cook for 5 minutes. Add tomato sauce and broth to a slow cooker. Add tomatoes with juice, beans, carrot mixture and corn, if using. Cover and cook on low setting for 8 hours. Add kale or spinach during the last hour of cooking, if using. Serves 6 to 8.

Bobbie Sofia
Lake Havasu City, AZ

A great healthy recipe to have in the fridge when family comes to visit... everyone loves it, and it's easy to get a bowlful anytime someone feels hungry!

Hearty Hominy Beef Stew

1 onion, chopped
2-lb. beef chuck roast, cubed
1/4 t. salt
1 green pepper, chopped
3 carrots, peeled and sliced
3 stalks celery, sliced
3 cloves garlic, minced
14-1/2 oz. can petite diced
    tomatoes
1 c. beef broth, divided
2 T. cornstarch
15-oz. can hominy, drained
    and rinsed

Place onion in a lightly greased slow cooker; top with beef. Sprinkle with salt. Add green pepper, carrots, celery and garlic to slow cooker. Pour tomatoes with juice and 3/4 cup broth over all. Cover and cook on low setting for 8 hours. In a bowl, mix together cornstarch and remaining broth until smooth; stir into slow cooker during the last 15 minutes of cooking. Stir in hominy and heat through. Serves 6.

87

Rita Morgan
Pueblo, CO

We like to top our soup with some sliced avocado for extra flavor and a little more creaminess.

The Easiest Rice Pudding

8 c. milk
1 c. long-cooking rice, uncooked
1 c. sugar
1/4 c. half-and-half
3 eggs
2 t. vanilla extract
1/2 t. cinnamon
1/4 t. salt

Spray a slow cooker with vegetable cooking spray; set aside. In a bowl, combine milk, rice and sugar; mix well. Spoon milk mixture into slow cooker. Cover and cook on low setting for 6 hours, or until rice is tender. When rice is tender, beat together eggs, half-and-half and remaining ingredients. Whisk 1/2 cup of milk mixture from slow cooker into egg mixture. Continue whisking in milk mixture, 1/2 cup at a time, until only half remains in slow cooker. Spoon everything back into slow cooker; stir. Cover and cook on low for 2 hours. Serves 8 to 10.

Barbara Rutan
Newport News, VA

We love old-fashioned rice pudding, and this version made in the slow cooker is so simple! We like to sprinkle a little bit of cinnamon and sweetened flaked coconut over ours for extra flavor.

Honeyed Apple Treat

4 tart apples, peeled, cored
   and sliced
2 c. granola with fruit and nuts
1/4 c. honey
2 T. butter, melted
1 t. cinnamon
1/2 t. nutmeg
Garnish: whipped topping,
   additional nutmeg

Combine apples and granola in a
slow cooker. In a separate bowl,
combine honey, butter, cinnamon
and nutmeg; pour over apple
mixture and mix well. Cover and
cook on low setting for 8 hours.
Garnish servings with a dollop of
whipped topping and sprinkle with
additional nutmeg. Serves 4 to 6.

89

Connie Bryant
Topeka, KS

This dessert is one my friend
Ellen shared with our family
when I was feeling a bit
under the weather. She
brought along a dozen fresh
eggs from her hens as well...
what a farmgirl!

Perfect Pepper Steak

1-1/2 to 2 lbs. beef round steak,
  sliced into strips
15-oz. can diced tomatoes
1 to 2 green and/or red peppers,
  sliced
1 onion, chopped
4-oz. can sliced mushrooms,
  drained
1/4 c. salsa
cooked rice

Combine all ingredients except rice in a freezer-safe container. Refrigerate overnight, or freeze until ready to use.

To cook:

Thaw beef mixture overnight in refrigerator if frozen; spoon into a slow cooker. Cover and cook on low setting for 6 to 8 hours. To serve, spoon over cooked rice. Makes 4 to 6 servings.

Stephanie Westfall
Dallas, GA

This recipe is one of my family's favorites! Sprinkle with chow mein noodles if you like a crunchy topping.

Swiss Steak Colorado Style

1-1/2 lb. beef chuck roast
15-oz. can diced tomatoes
1 c. red wine or beef broth
1 T. onion powder
1 t. garlic salt
1 t. pepper
2 carrots, peeled and sliced
1 onion, diced
1/2 to 1 c. beef broth
Optional: 1 T. cornstarch,
    1 T. water

Combine all ingredients except cornstarch and water in a freezer-safe container. Refrigerate overnight, or freeze until ready to use.

To cook:

Thaw beef mixture overnight in refrigerator if frozen; spoon into a slow cooker. Cover and cook on low setting for 5 to 6 hours. If a thicker consistency is desired, whisk together cornstarch and water in a cup; drizzle into beef mixture. Cook, uncovered, until thickened. Serves 4.

Roben Blakey
Westminster, CO

This is one of my husband's favorite go-to meals. We like to eat this as is, but sometimes we spoon it over a baked potato.

Meatless Mexican Chili

2 15-oz. cans ranch-style beans
2 10-oz. cans diced tomatoes
  with green chiles
15-1/2 oz. can white hominy,
  drained
15-1/2 oz. can golden hominy,
  drained
1-oz. pkg. ranch salad dressing
  mix
3 c. vegetable broth
Garnish: shredded Cheddar
  cheese, crushed tortilla chips

Combine all ingredients except
broth and garnish in a freezer-safe
container. Refrigerate overnight,
or freeze until ready to use.

To cook:

Thaw chili mixture overnight in
refrigerator if frozen; spoon into a
slow cooker. Stir in broth; cover and
cook on high setting for 6 hours, or
on low setting for 8 hours. Serve
individual portions sprinkled with
cheese and chips. Serves 6 to 8.

**Laura Witham
Anchorage, AK**

I sampled this chili while
visiting a friend of mine,
and I loved it so much I
asked for the recipe! I make
it whenever I need an easy
meal to feed a crowd.

Spicy Carnitas Tacos

2-lb. boneless pork loin, halved crosswise
1 onion, diced
3 carrots, peeled and diced
3 cloves garlic, minced
1 chipotle pepper in adobo sauce, chopped and 2 T. adobo sauce reserved
2 15-1/2 oz. cans cannellini beans, drained and rinsed
28-oz. can diced tomatoes
3 T. tomato paste
1-1/2 t. dried oregano
1 t. ground cumin
salt and pepper to taste
1/4 t. cinnamon
1/4 t. cayenne pepper
1/4 c. fresh cilantro, chopped
corn tortillas

Combine pork and all ingredients except tortillas in a freezer-safe container. Refrigerate overnight, or freeze until ready to use.

To cook:

Thaw pork mixture overnight in refrigerator if frozen; spoon into a slow cooker. Cover and cook on low setting for 8 hours. Remove pork and shred; return to slow cooker. Add cilantro; stir well. Serve in tortillas. Serves 8 to 10.

93

**Geneva Rogers
Gillette, WY**

We sprinkle ours with a little diced red onion, shredded cheese and a squeeze of lime juice.

Slow-Cooker Sausage-Stuffed Peppers

1 lb. ground pork sausage,
  browned and drained
1-1/2 c. cooked rice
1-1/2 c. salsa, divided
1-1/2 c. shredded Mexican-blend
  cheese, divided
1/2 t. salt
6 red, yellow and/or
  green peppers

Mix together sausage, rice, one cup salsa, one cup cheese and salt in a large bowl; set aside. Remove tops from peppers; remove seeds and discard tops. Stuff peppers evenly with sausage mixture. Individually wrap peppers in plastic wrap; place stuffed peppers in a freezer-safe container. Refrigerate overnight, or freeze until ready to use.

To cook:

Thaw peppers overnight in refrigerator if frozen. Spoon remaining 1/2 cup salsa into a lightly greased slow cooker. Unwrap peppers and stand up in slow cooker. Cover and cook on low setting for 4 to 5 hours, until peppers are tender. Sprinkle peppers with remaining cheese. Cover and cook for 5 to 10 minutes, until cheese is melted. Serves 6.

Cheri Maxwell
Gulf Breeze, FL

Stuffed peppers are a favorite in my household, so imagine how excited I was when a friend gave me this recipe to make them in the slow cooker!

Classic Spaghetti & Meatballs

1 lb. frozen cooked meatballs,
   thawed
26-oz. jar spaghetti sauce
1 onion, chopped
1-1/2 c. water
8-oz. pkg. spaghetti, uncooked
   and broken into 3-inch pieces
Garnish: grated Parmesan cheese

Combine meatballs, sauce and
onion in a freezer-safe container.
Refrigerate overnight, or freeze
until ready to use.

To cook:

Thaw meatball mixture overnight in
refrigerator if frozen; spoon into a
slow cooker. Add water; cover and
cook on low setting for 6 to 8 hours.
Stir well; add broken spaghetti. Turn
slow cooker to high setting. Cover
and cook for one additional hour,
stirring once during cooking, until
spaghetti is cooked. Top servings with
Parmesan cheese. Serves 4 to 6.

95

Susie Backus
Gooseberry Patch

Perfect pairing with a fresh
green salad from your garden
patch, or toast up some
thick & hearty slices of
garlic bread!

Cheesy Corn for a Crowd

4 15-1/4 oz. cans corn, drained
4 15-oz. cans creamed corn
8-oz. pkg. shredded Cheddar
   cheese
8-oz. pkg. shredded mozzarella
   cheese
2 8-1/2 oz. pkgs. corn muffin
   mix
4 eggs, beaten
16-oz. container French onion
   dip

Combine all ingredients except
dip in a freezer-safe container.
Refrigerate overnight, or freeze until
ready to use.

To cook:

Thaw corn mixture overnight in
refrigerator if frozen; spoon into a
lightly greased slow cooker. Stir dip
into corn mixture. Cover and cook
on high setting for 4-1/2 hours,
or on low setting for 9 hours.
Serves 15 to 18.

Jennifer Stacy
Hamler, OH

I make this yummy corn
casserole every time my
family gets together.
My nieces & nephews
can't get enough!

Meatloaf Made Easy

1 lb. ground pork sausage
1 lb. lean ground beef
1 onion, finely diced
2 c. shredded mozzarella cheese
1 c. dry bread crumbs
1 egg
1/2 c. milk
salt and pepper to taste
1 c. catsup
1/2 c. brown sugar

In a bowl, combine all ingredients except catsup and brown sugar. Form mixture into a rounded loaf; wrap in plastic wrap. Place loaf in a freeze-safe container. Refrigerate overnight, or freeze until ready to use.

To cook:

Thaw meatloaf overnight in refrigerator if frozen. Unwrap and place in a slow cooker; poke a few holes in the top of meatloaf with a skewer. In a bowl, stir together catsup and brown sugar. Spoon mixture over meatloaf. Cover and cook on low setting for 3 to 5 hours, until meatloaf is no longer pink in the center. Serves 6 to 8.

Aleta Mottet
Fairfield, IA

This is a recipe my husband loves and I think most men would. Leftovers can be served the next day, cold or reheated in a sandwich, and it's still yummy.

Easy Roast Beef Sandwiches

4 to 5-lb. beef chuck roast
0.7-oz. pkg. Italian salad
   dressing mix
8 to 10 pepperoncini peppers
2 c. water
16 to 20 sandwich buns
Garnish: brown mustard,
   roasted red pepper strips

Sprinkle roast with salad dressing mix; place in a freezer-safe container. Add peppers on top of roast. Refrigerate overnight, or freeze until ready to use.

To cook:

Thaw beef mixture overnight in refrigerator if frozen. Add beef and peppers to a slow cooker; pour in water. Cover and cook on low setting for 10 hours. Remove beef from slow cooker and shred; return shredded beef to juices in slow cooker. Serve shredded beef on buns; top with mustard and roasted red pepper strips. Makes 16 to 20 sandwiches.

Cynthia Holtz
Park Forest, IL

This recipe takes ten hours to cook, so turn it on first thing in the morning and forget about it until dinnertime.

Tuscan Beef Stew

2 lbs. stew beef cubes
2 to 3 T. oil
1/2 c. dry red wine or water
2 16-oz. cans cannellini beans, drained and rinsed
14-1/2 oz. can Italian-style diced tomatoes
3 carrots, peeled and cut into 1-inch pieces
1 t. Italian seasoning
1/2 t. garlic powder
15-oz. can tomato sauce
10-1/2 oz. can beef broth

In a large skillet over medium-high heat, cook beef in oil until no longer pink in the center; drain and cool. Combine beef and remaining ingredients except soup and broth in a freezer-safe container. Refrigerate overnight, or freeze until ready to use.

To cook:

Thaw beef mixture overnight in refrigerator if frozen; spoon into a slow cooker. Pour soup and broth over beef. Cover and cook on low setting for 8 to 9 hours. Serves 6.

Jean DePerna
Fairport, NY

One morning I tossed a few things together and this delicious dish was the result...I have been asked to make it ever since!

Split Pea Soup

1 lb. cooked ham, diced
1 lb. carrots, peeled and
  finely diced
1 onion, finely diced
2 12-oz. pkgs. dried split peas
salt and pepper to taste

Combine ham, carrots and onion
in a freezer-safe container.
Refrigerate overnight, or freeze
until ready to use.

To cook:

Thaw ham mixture overnight in
refrigerator if frozen. Combine
thawed ham mixture and dried peas
in a slow cooker. Add enough water
to cover. Cover and cook on high
setting for 6 to 8 hours, stirring
occasionally, until peas are tender
and soup becomes very thick. Add
additional water to reach desired
consistency, if desired; season with
salt and pepper. Serves 8 to 10.

Krista Marshall
Fort Wayne, IN

My husband is a pretty
amazing cook. He has a
few recipes that are his
signature dishes, and this
is one of them.

Orange-Glazed Chicken

6 boneless, skinless chicken
   breasts
6-oz. can frozen orange juice
   concentrate, partially thawed
1 onion, diced
1 clove garlic, minced
1/2 t. dried rosemary
salt and pepper to taste
1/4 c. cold water
2 T. cornstarch

Combine chicken, orange juice,
onion, garlic and rosemary in a
freezer-safe container. Refrigerate
overnight, or freeze until ready
to use.

To cook:

Thaw chicken mixture overnight in
refrigerator if frozen; spoon into a
slow cooker; season with salt and
pepper. Cover and cook on low
setting for 7 to 9 hours. Remove
chicken from slow cooker; keep
warm. In a bowl, mix together water
and cornstarch; drizzle into juices
in slow cooker. Partially cover slow
cooker; cook on high setting until
sauce is thick and bubbly, about 15 to
30 minutes. Serve sauce with sliced
chicken. Serves 6.

101

Anna McMaster
Portland, OR

I love the tangy zip of
this chicken when it's
served over a bed of
crisp salad greens.

Slow-Cooker Tagine Chicken

2 lbs. boneless, skinless chicken
   breasts, cubed
1 T. ground coriander
1 T. paprika
1 T. ground cumin
1 t. turmeric
1/8 t. cinnamon
1 c. onion, diced
3/4 c. water
3/4 c. raisins
3/4 c. prunes
14-oz. can chicken broth
cooked couscous

In a bowl, toss chicken with spices.
Combine chicken, onion, water,
raisins and prunes in a freezer-safe
container. Refrigerate overnight,
or freeze until ready to use.

To cook:

Thaw chicken mixture overnight in
refrigerator if frozen; spoon into a
slow cooker. Pour in broth; cover and
cook on low setting for 8 to 9 hours.
Serve over couscous. Serves 4.

Liz Plotnick-Snay
Gooseberry Patch

My husband and I love to
try all different types
of food...Thai, Indian,
Lebanese, you name it.
We both really enjoyed
this tasty dish.

Chicken Cacciatore

4 boneless, skinless chicken
  breasts
28-oz. can crushed tomatoes
14-oz. can tomato sauce
1 onion, grated
2 bay leaves
2 t. dried oregano
1 t. dried basil
1 t. garlic powder
Optional: 1/2 c. dry sherry
cooked spaghetti
Garnish: grated Parmesan cheese

Combine all ingredients except
spaghetti and garnish in a freezer-
safe container. Refrigerate overnight,
or freeze until ready to use.

To cook:

Thaw chicken mixture overnight in
refrigerator if frozen; spoon into a
slow cooker. Cover and cook on
high setting for one hour. Turn slow
cooker to low setting and cook for
6 to 8 hours more. Remove lid
during last hour of cooking to allow
sauce to thicken. Discard bay leaves.
Serve chicken mixture over spaghetti;
garnish servings with Parmesan
cheese. Serves 4.

103

Marlene Huellen
Carnegie, PA
Really easy and really tasty.
Plus, since you use the slow
cooker, that means dinner is
ready when you are.

Collins' Best Lentil & Sausage Soup

1 lb. Kielbasa turkey sausage,
   cut into 1/2-inch pieces
1 c. onion, chopped
1 c. celery, chopped
1 c. carrots, peeled and chopped
1 c. redskin potatoes, diced
2 T. fresh flat-leaf parsley,
   chopped
1/2 t. pepper
1/8 t. ground nutmeg
6 c. beef broth
1 c. dried lentils, rinsed
   and drained

Combine all ingredients except broth and lentils in a freezer-safe container. Refrigerate overnight, or freeze until ready to use.

To cook:

Thaw sausage mixture overnight in refrigerator if frozen. Combine soup mixture with broth and dried lentils in a slow cooker. Cover and cook on low setting for 6 to 8 hours; stir before serving. Serves 6 to 8.

Michelle Collins
San Diego, CA
A very good friend of mine who passed away used to make a lentil sausage soup that I adored, so whenever I make this, I think of him.

Sweet & Spicy Roast Beef

3 to 4-lb. bottom-round
  beef roast
12-oz. can beer or non-alcoholic
  beer
1 c. catsup
1/4 c. brown sugar, packed
3 T. all-purpose flour
1 T. prepared horseradish,
  or to taste
1 T. garlic powder
1 t. pepper
1 onion, sliced

Combine all ingredients except
onion in a freezer-safe container.
Refrigerate overnight, or freeze
until ready to use.

To cook:

Thaw beef mixture overnight in
refrigerator if frozen. Place onion
in a lightly greased slow cooker;
spoon thawed beef mixture over
onion. Cover and cook on low setting
for 8 to 10 hours. Remove roast from
slow cooker and slice; serve topped
with sauce from slow cooker.
Serves 8 to 10.

105

Brenda Bodnar
Mayfield Village, OH
I've been making this for
years...the heavenly smell
of the slow-simmering beef
warms heart & soul and
piques the appetite.

Tomato & Artichoke Chicken

4 boneless, skinless chicken
   breasts
3 T. Italian salad dressing
1 t. Italian seasoning
1/2 onion, very thinly sliced
4 cloves garlic, minced
14-1/2 oz. can diced tomatoes,
   drained
14-oz. can quartered artichoke
   hearts, drained
2 to 3 T. dried parsley
cooked spaghetti

Combine all ingredients except
spaghetti in a freezer-safe container.
Refrigerate overnight, or freeze until
ready to use.

To cook:

Thaw chicken mixture overnight in
refrigerator if frozen; spoon into a
slow cooker. Cover and cook on low
setting for 4 to 5 hours, until chicken
juices run clear. To serve, spoon
chicken mixture over cooked
spaghetti. Serves 4 to 6.

Rachel Boyd
Defiance, OH

This is one of the best
summer recipes I've seen.
The flavor of the artichokes
pairs really well with
the tomatoes!

Chocolate Peanut Clusters

2 16-oz. jars salted dry-roasted
   peanuts
32-oz. pkg. white melting
   chocolate, chopped
12-oz. pkg. semi-sweet chocolate
   chips
4-oz. pkg. sweet baking
   chocolate, chopped

Combine all ingredients in a slow
cooker. Cover and cook on low
setting for 1-1/2 hours. Turn off
slow cooker. Let stand 20 minutes;
stir until blended. Drop by rounded
tablespoonfuls onto wax paper. Let
stand one hour, or until firm. Store
clusters in an airtight container,
or freeze for up to one month.
Makes 4 dozen.

107

Christi Assink
South Haven, MI
A tasty and easy recipe
for seasonal gift giving!
A cookie scoop makes the
job go even faster.

INDEX

INDEX

Mains (Veggie & Seafood)

Sides

Soups, Chilis & Stews

Super-Easy Sausage Sandwiches, page 37

Crockery Apple Pie, page 59

Mike's Irresistible Italian Chops, page 15

Herb Garden Chicken, page 67

Our Story

Back in 1984, we were next-door neighbors raising our families in the little town of Delaware, Ohio. Two moms with small children, we were looking for a way to do what we loved and stay home with the kids too. We had always shared a love of home cooking and making memories with family & friends and so, after many a conversation over the backyard fence, **Gooseberry Patch** was born.

We put together our first catalog at our kitchen tables, enlisting the help of our loved ones wherever we could. From that very first mailing, we found an immediate connection with many of our customers and it wasn't long before we began receiving letters, photos and recipes from these new friends. In 1992, we put together our very first cookbook, compiled from hundreds of these recipes and, the rest, as they say, is history.

Hard to believe it's been over 30 years since those kitchen-table days! From that original little **Gooseberry Patch** family, we've grown to include an amazing group of creative folks who love cooking, decorating and creating as much as we do. Today, we're best known for our homestyle, family-friendly cookbooks, now recognized as national bestsellers.

JoAnn & Vickie

One thing's for sure, we couldn't have done it without our friends all across the country. Each year, we're honored to turn thousands of your recipes into our collectible cookbooks. Our hope is that each book captures the stories and heart of all of you who have shared with us. Whether you've been with us since the beginning or are just discovering us, welcome to the **Gooseberry Patch** family!

Visit us online:
www.gooseberrypatch.com
1•800•854•6673

U.S. to Metric Recipe Equivalents

Volume Measurements

1/4 teaspoon	1 mL
1/2 teaspoon	2 mL
1 teaspoon	5 mL
1 tablespoon = 3 teaspoons	15 mL
2 tablespoons = 1 fluid ounce	30 mL
1/4 cup	60 mL
1/3 cup	75 mL
1/2 cup = 4 fluid ounces	125 mL
1 cup = 8 fluid ounces	250 mL
2 cups = 1 pint =16 fluid ounces	500 mL
4 cups = 1 quart	1 L

Weights

1 ounce	30 g
4 ounces	120 g
8 ounces	225 g
16 ounces = 1 pound	450 g

Oven Temperatures

300° F	150° C
325° F	160° C
350° F	180° C
375° F	190° C
400° F	200° C
450° F	230° C

Baking Pan Sizes

Square

8x8x2 inches	2 L = 20x20x5 cm
9x9x2 inches	2.5 L = 23x23x5 cm

Rectangular

13x9x2 inches	3.5 L = 33x23x5 cm

Loaf

9x5x3 inches	2 L = 23x13x7 cm

Round

8x1-1/2 inches	1.2 L = 20x4 cm
9x1-1/2 inches	1.5 L = 23x4 cm

Recipe Abbreviations

t. = teaspoon	ltr. = liter
T. = tablespoon	oz. = ounce
c. = cup	lb. = pound
pt. = pint	doz. = dozen
qt. = quart	pkg. = package
gal. = gallon	env. = envelope

Kitchen Measurements

A pinch = 1/8 tablespoon	1 fluid ounce = 2 tablespoons
3 teaspoons = 1 tablespoon	4 fluid ounces = 1/2 cup
2 tablespoons = 1/8 cup	8 fluid ounces = 1 cup
4 tablespoons = 1/4 cup	16 fluid ounces = 1 pint
8 tablespoons = 1/2 cup	32 fluid ounces = 1 quart
16 tablespoons = 1 cup	16 ounces net weight = 1 pound
2 cups = 1 pint	
4 cups = 1 quart	
4 quarts = 1 gallon	